First World War

and Army of Occupation

War Diary

France, Belgium and Germany

21 DIVISION
Divisional Troops
Royal Army Medical Corps
Divisional Field Ambulance Workshop Unit
1 October 1915 - 31 March 1916

WO95/2148/2

The Naval & Military Press Ltd
www.nmarchive.com
Published in association with The National Archives

Published by

The Naval & Military Press Ltd

Unit 10 Ridgewood Industrial Park,

Uckfield, East Sussex,

TN22 5QE England

Tel: +44 (0) 1825 749494

www.naval-military-press.com

www.nmarchive.com

This diary has been reprinted in facsimile from the original. Any imperfections are inevitably reproduced and the quality may fall short of modern type and cartographic standards.

Contents

Document type	Place/Title	Date From	Date To
Heading	WO95/2148/2 Div. Field Ambulance Workshop Unit		
Heading	21st Division 21st Fd Amb. Workshop Unit Oct 1915-Mar 1916		
Heading	21st Division 21st F.A.W.U. Vol 2 Oct 15		
War Diary	Lietres	01/10/1915	01/10/1915
War Diary	Morbeques	02/10/1915	02/10/1915
War Diary	Andeghem	03/10/1915	06/10/1915
War Diary	Merris	07/10/1915	31/10/1915
Heading	21st Division 21st D.F.A.W.V. Vol. 2 Nov 15		
War Diary	Merris	01/11/1915	12/11/1915
War Diary	Nieppe	12/11/1915	23/11/1915
War Diary	Pont Nieppe	24/11/1915	30/11/1915
Heading	21st F.A. W. O Vol 4 December 1915		
War Diary	Pont De Nieppe	01/12/1915	31/12/1915
Heading	21st F.A.W.U. Vol 5 Jan 16		
War Diary	Pont De Nieppe	01/01/1916	31/01/1916
Heading	21st F.A.W.U Feb 1916		
Heading	21st Division F.A.W Vol 6		
War Diary	Pont De Nieppe	01/02/1916	29/02/1916
Heading	21st Div F.A.W.U Vol 7 March 1916		
War Diary	Pont De Nieppe	01/03/1916	22/03/1916
War Diary	Merris	23/03/1916	31/03/1916

WO95

2148/2

Div. Field Ambulance
Workshop Unit.

21ST DIVISION

21ST FD AMB.WORKSHOP UNIT

OCT 1915 - MAR 1916

21st Division

121/7608

F

Q

21st D. A. W. D.

Vol 2

Oct 15

Mar 16

nil

Cm

Army Form C. 2118

Instructions regarding War Diaries and Intelligence Summaries are contained in F. S. Regs., Part II. and the Staff Manual respectively. Title Pages will be prepared in manuscript.

WAR DIARY
or
INTELLIGENCE SUMMARY
(Erase heading not required.)

Place	Date	Hour	Summary of Events and Information	Remarks and references to Appendices
Liettres	1/10/15.		Moved from Liettres to Morbecque with Division	
Morbecque	2/10/15		" " Morbecque to Hondeghem (near Hazebrouck) where Division is now stationed.	
Hondeghem	3/10/15		Work in progress. Visited Field Ambulances &c.	
"	4/10/15		" " " Visited Field Ambulances &c	
"	5/10/15		" " "	
"	6/10/15		Moved from Hondeghem to Merris	
Merris	7/10/15		Rigged up Workshops &c. Work in progress.	
"	8/10/15 to		Work in progress, overhauling all	
"	13/10/15		Ambulances & getting organised.	
"	14/10/15 to		Workshop settled down & all	
Merris	31/10/15.		work fully in hand. Nothing special to report.	

[illegible signature]
~~OFFICER COMMANDING,~~
21st I. A. W.

21st Division

21st D.A.D.V.S. (?)

~~H.Q. 21st Div.~~

Vol: 2

Q

F

121
7624

Nov 15.

Army Form C. 2118.

Instructions regarding War Diaries and Intelligence Summaries are contained in F. S. Regs., Part II. and the Staff Manual respectively. Title Pages will be prepared in manuscript.

WAR DIARY
or
INTELLIGENCE SUMMARY
(Erase heading not required.)

Place	Date	Hour	Summary of Events and Information	Remarks and references to Appendices
Merris to	1/11/15		Work in hand. Nothing of a special character to report.	
	11/11/15		Preparing to move with the Division.	
Merris	12/11/15	9 a.m.	Ready to move.	
"	" "	10 a.m.	Moved off to Armentieres via Bailleul & Nieppe	
Nieppe	" "	12 a.m.	Waited until position found in Armentieres for Shops.	
Armentieres	" "	2 p.m.	Moved into Armentieres & took up new position in D.H.Q's.	
"	" "	10 p.m. to 12 p.m.	Huns began strafing badly, the billet which was occupied by my men was hit but no one hurt cellars taken to in great haste. My own billet was hit by a H.E. since discovered to be a 5.9, an R.A.M.C. officer sleeping next to me was wounded in the head, roof, walls & ceiling were all	

1875 Wt. W593/826 1,000,000 4/15 J.B.C. & A. A.D.S.S./Forms/C. 2118.

Army Form C. 2118

Instructions regarding War Diaries and Intelligence Summaries are contained in F. S. Regs., Part II. and the Staff Manual respectively. Title Pages will be prepared in manuscript.

WAR DIARY
or
INTELLIGENCE SUMMARY
(Erase heading not required.)

Place	Date	Hour	Summary of Events and Information	Remarks and references to Appendices
			smashed in, luckily I was not in [illegible] & got off with a severe shaking & one or two bruises, a very lucky escape, after half an hour or so we got some soldiers to hear our calls, they smashed the front door in & after some time arrived in the wreckage with a light, we got out safely & I accompanied Whitfield (Lt) to the F.A where he was dressed & I now understand he is at a C.C.S.	
			I finished the night in the ground floor of another billet.	
Armentières	12/11/15 to 17/11/15		Nothing unusual occurred, our guns were firing pretty frequently. Work well in hand at Shops.	
"	18/11/15		Another strafe by the Huns luckily in the daytime enemy [illegible] to the cellars until after dark, when the firing ceased, only a few people wounded; we then gave the Huns a severe retaliation, which I understand had great effect.	

1875 Wt. W593/826 1,000,000 4/15 J.B.C. & A. A.D.S.S./Forms/C. 2118.

Army Form C. 2[illegible]

Instructions regarding War Diaries and Intelligence Summaries are contained in F. S. Regs., Part II. and the Staff Manual respectively. Title Pages will be prepared in manuscript.

WAR DIARY
or
INTELLIGENCE SUMMARY
(Erase heading not required.)

Place	Date	Hour	Summary of Events and Information	Remarks and references to Appendices
Armentières	18/11/15 to		Work well in progress, no further shelling on the	
"	23/11/15		part of the Germans.	
Pont Nieppe	24/11/15		Received orders to move to Pont Nieppe, I have now	
			part of my Workshops here, all work well in	
	to		hand & a little further away from the Shells.	
	30/11/15		Nothing of a special nature to report.	

[illegible signature]
OFFICER COMMANDING, M.T.
21st D. A. W.
21st Division.

1875 Wt. W593/826 1,000,000 4/15 J.B.C. & A. A.D.S.S./Forms/C. 2118.

F

December 1915

21st F.A. W.O.

Vol: 4

121

7935

3/12/15

Army Form C. 2118

Instructions regarding War Diaries and Intelligence Summaries are contained in F. S. Regs., Part II. and the Staff Manual respectively. Title Pages will be prepared in manuscript.

WAR DIARY
or
INTELLIGENCE SUMMARY

(Erase heading not required.)

Place	Date	Hour	Summary of Events and Information	Remarks and references to Appendices
Pont de Nieppe	1/12/15 to 31/12/15.		Nothing of a special character to report whatsoever, all work well in hand, ambulances are standing up to the work very well indeed.	

Howard. Godfrey Lt.
OFFICER COMMANDING
21ST DIV.:—F. A. W.

1875 Wt. W593/826 1,000,000 4/15 J.B.C. & A. A.D.S.S./Forms/C. 2118.

Jan '16

F

21st F.A.W.U.
Vol: 5

Instructions regarding War Diaries and Intelligence Summaries are contained in F. S. Regs., Part II. and the Staff Manual respectively. Title Pages will be prepared in manuscript.

WAR DIARY
or
INTELLIGENCE SUMMARY

(Erase heading not required.)

Army Form C. 2118

Place	Date	Hour	Summary of Events and Information	Remarks and references to Appendices
Pont de Nieppe	Jan. 1st 1916 to Jan. 31st 1916.		Everything proceeding very quietly, nothing of a special character to note. All work on Ambulances well in hand. Cars standing up to the work very well indeed.	

Howard Godfrey Capt

OFFICER COMMANDING
21ST DIV.:—F. A. W.

Feb 1916

2/d. Y. a. W. U.

21st. Division RAW
Vol. 6.

Instructions regarding War Diaries and Intelligence Summaries are contained in F. S. Regs., Part II. and the Staff Manual respectively. Title Pages will be prepared in manuscript.

WAR DIARY
or
INTELLIGENCE SUMMARY
(Erase heading not required.)

Army Form C. 2118

Place	Date	Hour	Summary of Events and Information	Remarks and references to Appendices
Pont de Nieppe	1/2/16		Returned from my 8 days leave, found everything quite satisfactory	
"	2/2/16		Examined all orders & correspondence during my leave	
"	3/2/16		Proceeded & examined 63rd & 64th F.A. cars, found 64th cars in very bad condition, issued strong complaints, hope to be rectified in future	
"	4/2/16		Decision arrived at re award of winner for "Challenge Cup". The 64th M.T. N.C.O's & men won same. This cup is given for general efficiency each month. All work well in hand.	
"	5/2/16 to 9/2/16		All work well in hand. Nothing of a special nature to report.	
"	10/2/16		" " " " "	
"	11/2/16		Armentieres shelled pretty heavily, shells going over workshop	

Instructions regarding War Diaries and Intelligence Summaries are contained in F. S. Regs., Part II. and the Staff Manual respectively. Title Pages will be prepared in manuscript.

WAR DIARY
or
INTELLIGENCE SUMMARY
(Erase heading not required.)

Army Form C. 2118

Place	Date	Hour	Summary of Events and Information	Remarks and references to Appendices
Pont de Nieppe		12/2/16.	Work well in hand, Pont de Nieppe hit by a H.E. (slight panic amongst the inhabitants). Shells dropping away near the Pont, hardly any damage done to bridge.	
		13/2/16	Shell landed about 50 yds from shops, (H.E. Shrapnel) evidently fired at incorrectly as it only went on percussion.	
" "		14/2/16 to 16/2/16	No more shelling, work well in hand.	
Pont de Nieppe		16/2/16 to 29/2/16.	No news of a special character to report, all work well in hand, usual inspections carried out.	

OFFICER COMMANDING
21ST DIV.:—F. A. W.

1875 Wt. W593/826 1,000,000 4/15 J.B.C. & A. A.D.S.S./Forms/C. 2118.

21st D W
F.A.W. U.
Vol 7

March 1916.

Army Form C. 2118

Instructions regarding War Diaries and Intelligence Summaries are contained in F. S. Regs., Part II. and the Staff Manual respectively. Title Pages will be prepared in manuscript.

WAR DIARY
or
INTELLIGENCE SUMMARY
(Erase heading not required.)

Place	Date	Hour	Summary of Events and Information	Remarks and references to Appendices
Pont de Nieppe	1/3/16		All work on M.T. Ambulances well in hand, nothing to report regarding anything of an unusual character.	
to				
"	22/3/16			
Merris	23/3/16		Orders received to proceed to Merris, the division are going into rest.	
"	24/3/16		Shops again set up & all work again put in hand.	
"	31/3/16			

[illegible]
OFFICER COMMANDING
21ST DIV.:—F. A. W.

1875 Wt. W593/826 1,000,000 4/15 J.B.C. & A. A.D.S.S./Forms/C. 2118.

www.ingramcontent.com/pod-product-compliance
Lightning Source LLC
Chambersburg PA
CBHW081252170426
43191CB00037B/2128

9781474512084